THE
CAT BUTT

Coloring & Activity Book

Library of Congress Cataloging-in-Publication Data:

Names: Brains, Val, author.
Title: The cat butt coloring & activity book / Val Brains.
Other titles: Cat butt coloring and activity book
Description: San Francisco : Chronicle Books, [2020].
Identifiers: LCCN 2019048981 | ISBN 9781452184548 (paperback)
Subjects: LCSH: Cats—Pictorial works. | Cats—Miscellanea. | Coloring
books—Specimens. | BISAC: GAMES & ACTIVITIES / Coloring Books
Classification: LCC SF446 .B6774 2020 | DDC 636.8022/2—dc23
LC record available at https://lccn.loc.gov/2019048981

Manufactured in China.

Illustrations by Val Brains.

10

Chronicle books and gifts are available at special quantity
discounts to corporations, professional associations, literacy
programs, and other organizations. For details and discount
information, please contact our premiums department at
corporatesales@chroniclebooks.com or at 1-800-759-0190.

Chronicle Books LLC
680 Second Street
San Francisco, CA 94107
www.chroniclebooks.com

THE CAT BUTT

Coloring & Activity Book

Val Brains

CHRONICLE BOOKS

SAN FRANCISCO

WORD SEARCH

```
B C O R N I S H R E X A R S V
H L H C O H D A F I C H U T J
D I N A P O L E O N O S R K
L B M T O D S T I B U L S A F
O R I A H T R O H S N F I N G
F E G O L S E L T A I T A N O
H A R D F A W X I O G Q N O F
S P E L K J Y N B L T M B O I
I S P E R S I A N I K J L C G
T N Z I T S D O N L E Z U E T
T G A J S S P H Y N X P E N S
O N P Y Z U C C F E L N D I N
C D B E H J L A G N E B A A M
S A W O P I N G M A F O R M U
```

WORD BOX:

Russian Blue	Napoleon	Scottish Fold	Maine Coon
Himalayan	Bengal	Persian	Manx
Shorthair	Sphynx	Cornish Rex	Abyssinian

BONUS Q: What do all the words you found have in common?

CONNECT - THE - DOTS

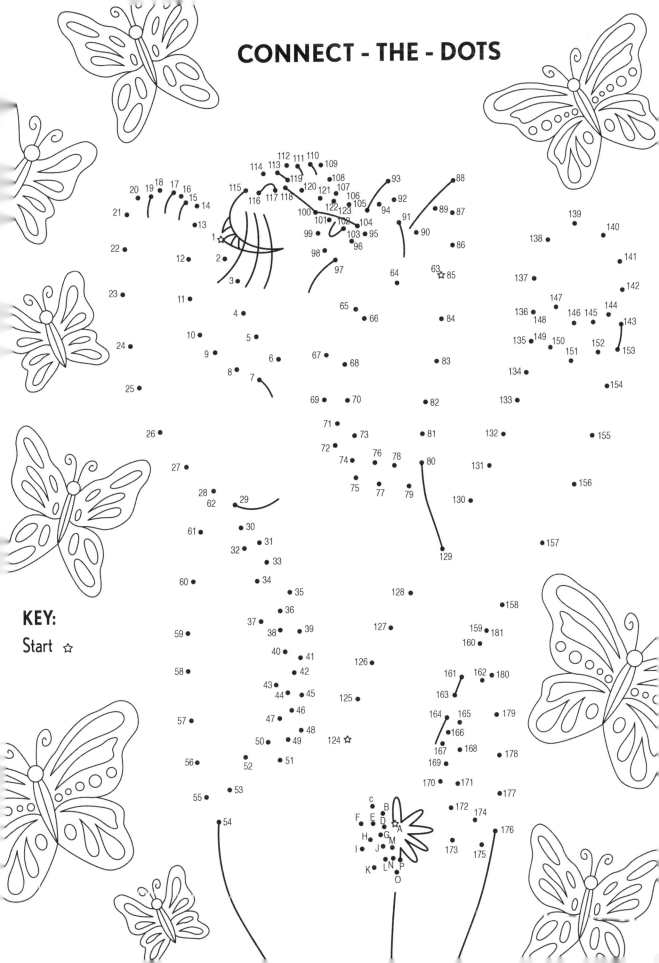

KEY:

Start ☆

WHAT'S DIFFERENT?

HINT: There are 8 differences to find!

CAT BUTT GLASSES!

STEP 1: Color your
cat butt glasses!

STEP 2: Cut out
the glasses and temples.

STEP 3: Attach the
temples behind the dotted
lines, fold the wings over
them, and secure with some
clear tape.

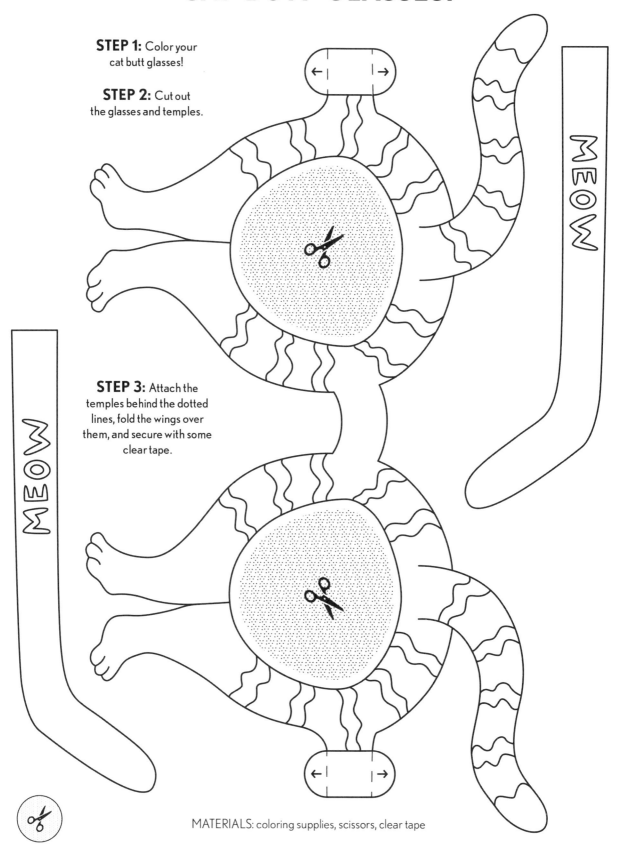

MEOW

MEOW

MATERIALS: coloring supplies, scissors, clear tape

CAT BUTT GLASSES to share!

STEP 1: Color your cat butt glasses!

STEP 2: Cut out the glasses and temples.

STEP 3: Attach the temples behind the dotted lines, fold the wings over them, and secure with some clear tape.

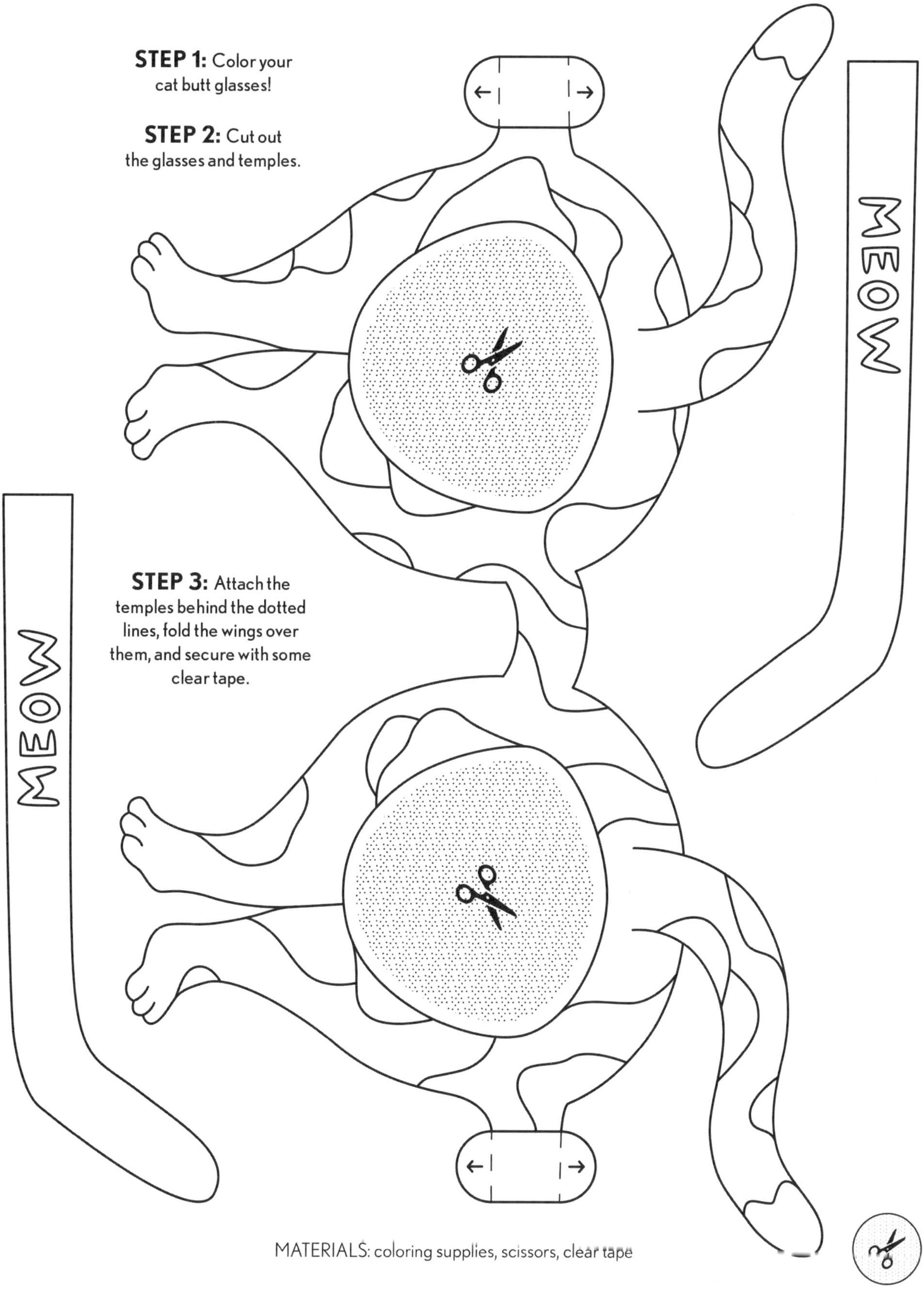

MEOW

MEOW

MATERIALS: coloring supplies, scissors, clear tape

CAT WORD

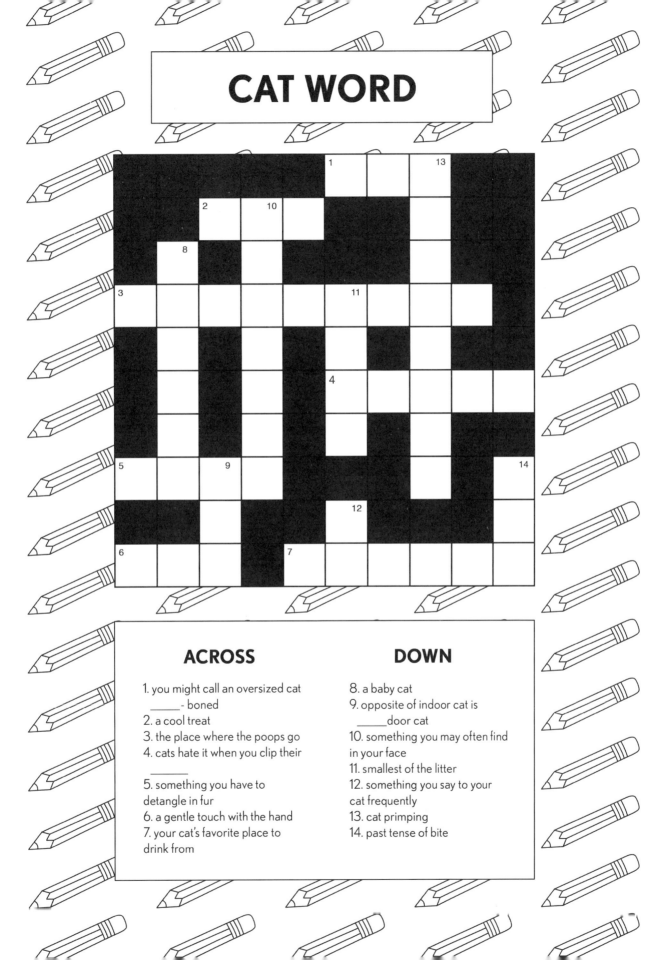

ACROSS

1. you might call an oversized cat
   _____ - boned
2. a cool treat
3. the place where the poops go
4. cats hate it when you clip their

   _____
5. something you have to
   detangle in fur
6. a gentle touch with the hand
7. your cat's favorite place to
   drink from

DOWN

8. a baby cat
9. opposite of indoor cat is
   _____ door cat
10. something you may often find
    in your face
11. smallest of the litter
12. something you say to your
    cat frequently
13. cat primping
14. past tense of bite

CAT BUTT BOOKMARKS

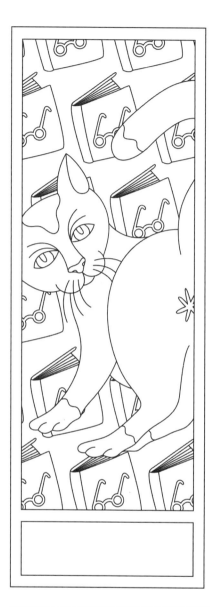

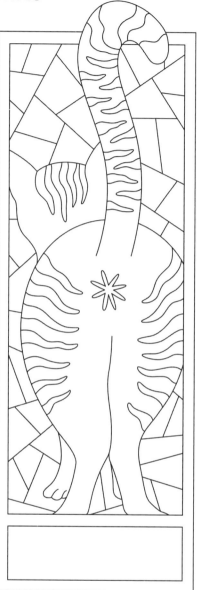

STEP 1:
Color the cat bookmarks.

STEP 2:
Cut them out.

STEP 3:
Use them with your favorite books!

MATERIALS:
coloring supplies, scissors

FILL - IN - THE - CAT

Use your imagination to draw the rest of the cat!

MAZE

CAKE STENCIL INSTRUCTIONS

MATERIALS:

- minimum 9 inch (23 cm) round cake pan (or you can use a larger rectangular pan)
- cake mix, ingredients, and recipe
- powdered sugar
- fine mesh strainer
- small sharp scissors (like makeup scissors)

STEP 1
Cut out only the dotted fill sections and discard. Leave the sheet of paper as an intact rectangle.

STEP 2
Mix and bake the cake of your choice according to your recipe or box instructions. We recommend a chocolate or dyed cake for maximum constrast with the powdered sugar. Once the cake has fully cooled to the touch, arrange the cat butt design on top of it.

STEP 3
Using the fine mesh strainer, sift powdered sugar over the cat butt design until the powdered sugar creates a solid layer on the cake.

STEP 4
Gently peel the stencil up from the cake.

STEP 5
Share and enjoy!

CAKE STENCIL

CAKE STENCIL

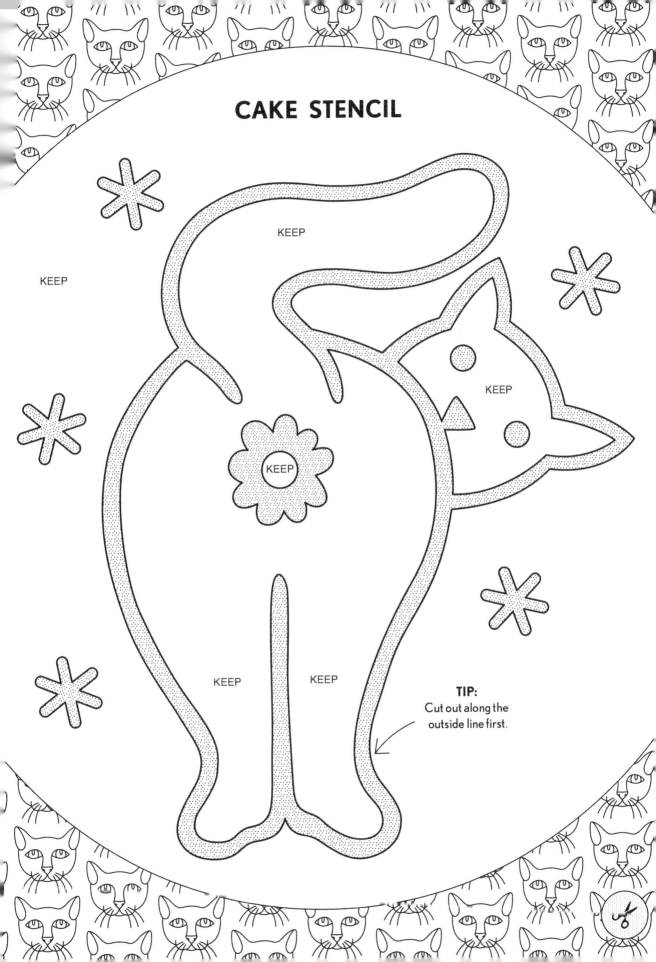

KEEP

KEEP

KEEP

KEEP

KEEP

KEEP

TIP:
Cut out along the
outside line first.

WORD SEARCH

Y	H	A	B	Z	K	C	F	I	E	C	P	F	K	A
R	S	Y	O	W	L	J	M	Y	N	I	B	O	L	E
V	E	Q	T	O	G	H	S	G	A	P	S	G	U	M
I	K	T	R	E	F	S	P	U	R	R	N	J	A	H
B	C	A	T	M	N	O	C	X	R	I	G	V	W	Y
M	H	I	F	A	L	K	S	S	I	H	U	A	R	C
O	V	C	R	O	H	M	G	K	P	C	O	P	E	X
A	T	L	A	G	T	C	L	U	Y	T	R	O	T	M
L	K	M	I	L	L	I	R	T	F	E	J	E	A	K
X	O	J	Y	A	U	R	S	O	G	Y	L	M	C	T
A	D	I	N	F	I	V	N	E	R	R	X	S	U	H
N	X	S	Z	H	O	Y	J	I	N	D	O	C	Q	I
D	F	D	C	A	G	S	C	R	E	A	M	W	P	M
I	O	N	S	O	K	P	B	A	L	M	F	U	L	T

(12 words)

WORD BOX:

Chatter	Hiss	Caterwaul	Chirp
Meow	Snarl	Purr	Scream
Trill	Yowl	Growl	Chirrup

BONUS Q: What do all the words you found have in common?

CONNECT - THE - DOTS

KEY:

Start ☆

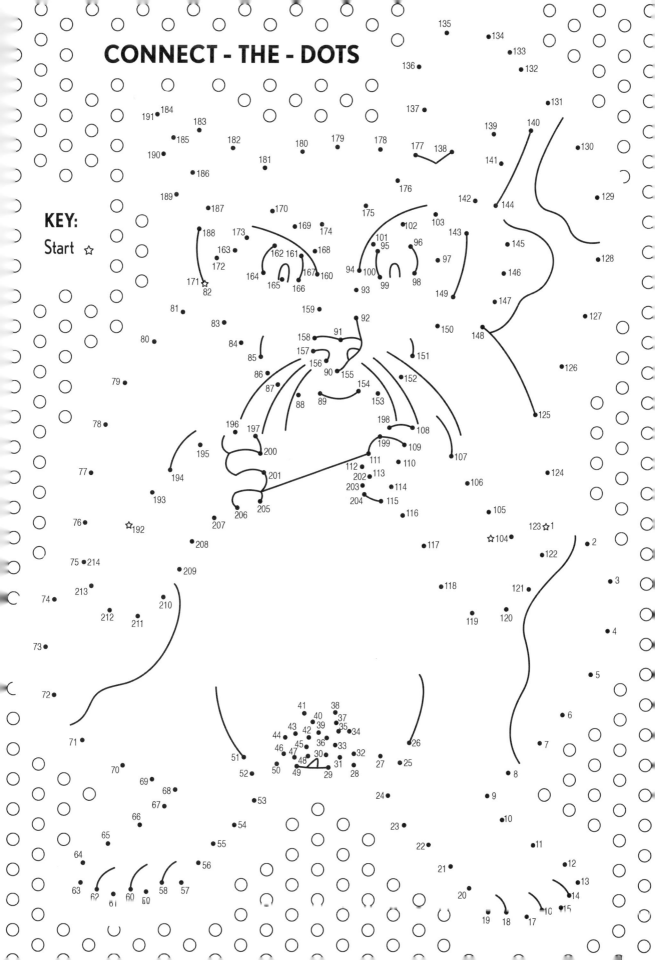

WORD SCRAMBLE

1. RUYO EFAC   _ _ _ _   _ _ _ _

2. DINOSLWLIW   _ _ _ _ _ _ _ _ _

3. HITENCK LEBAT   _ _ _ _ _ _ _   _ _ _ _ _

4. MUTREPOC   _ _ _ _ _ _ _ _

5. HUCOC   _ _ _ _ _

6. NI HET RIA   _ _   _ _ _   _ _ _

7. TRETNUCOOP   _ _ _ _ _ _ _ _ _ _

8. OURY TELPA   _ _ _ _   _ _ _ _ _

9. WOILPL   _ _ _ _ _ _

10. DRABROCAD XBO   _ _ _ _ _ _ _ _ _   _ _ _

HINT: These are all things your cat likes to put its butt on!

CAT WORD

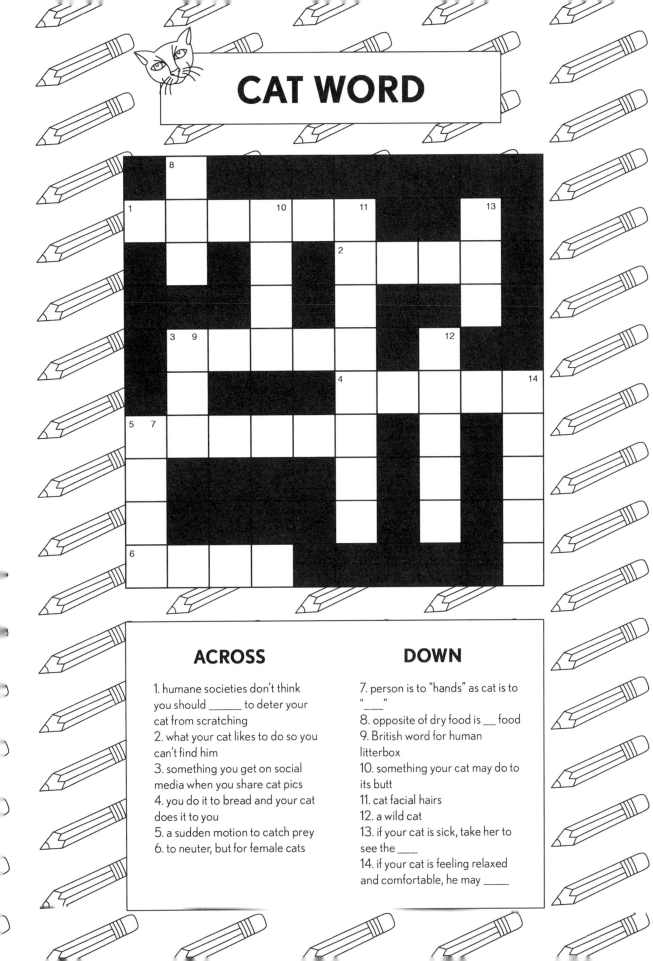

ACROSS

1. humane societies don't think you should _____ to deter your cat from scratching
2. what your cat likes to do so you can't find him
3. something you get on social media when you share cat pics
4. you do it to bread and your cat does it to you
5. a sudden motion to catch prey
6. to neuter, but for female cats

DOWN

7. person is to "hands" as cat is to "____"
8. opposite of dry food is __ food
9. British word for human litterbox
10. something your cat may do to its butt
11. cat facial hairs
12. a wild cat
13. if your cat is sick, take her to see the ___
14. if your cat is feeling relaxed and comfortable, he may _____

WHAT'S DIFFERENT?

HINT:
There are 8
differences
to find!

MAZE

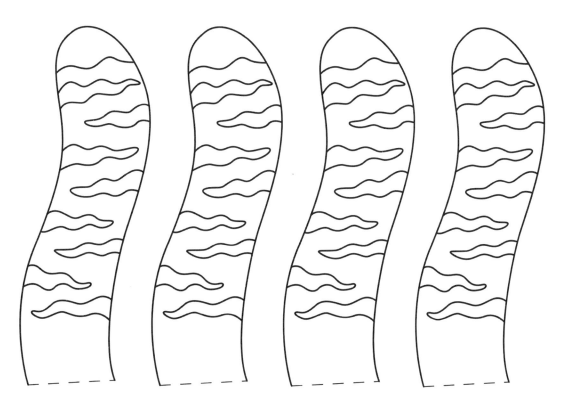

STEP 1

Color each tail uniqely and cut each out.

STEP 2

Attach tape to the back of each tail.

STEP 3

Tape the tail-less cat up on the wall.

STEP 4

Blindfold and spin your tail pinners.

STEP 5

Try to pin the tail on the cat butt!

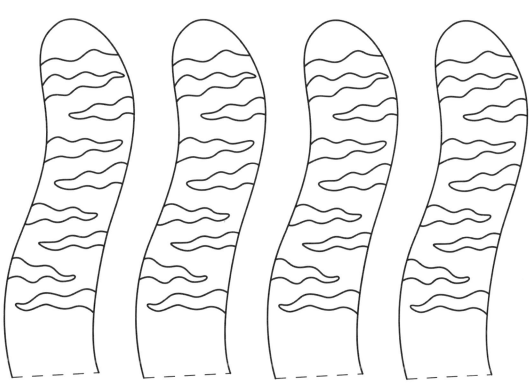

PIN THE BUTT ON THE CAT!

MATERIALS: coloring supplies, scissors, wall-safe tape, blindfold (bandana or scarf)

TIP:
Cut just
inside the
dotted line.

STEP 1	**STEP 2**	**STEP 3**	**STEP 4**	**STEP 5**
Color each hole uniqely and cut each out.	Attach tape to the back of each hole.	Tape the hole-less cat up on the wall.	Blindfold and spin your hole pinners.	Try to pin the hole on the cat butt!

SOLUTIONS

CAT WORD 1

ACROSS	DOWN
1. big	8. kitten
2. ice	9. out
3. litterbox	10. catbutt
4. nails	11. runt
5. knot	12. no
6. pet	13. grooming
7. toilet	14. bit

CAT WORD 2

ACROSS	DOWN
1. declaw	7. paws
2. hide	8. wet
3. likes	9. loo
4. knead	10. lick
5. pounce	11. whiskers
6. spay	12. feral
	13. vet
	14. drool

SOLUTIONS

WORD SEARCH 1

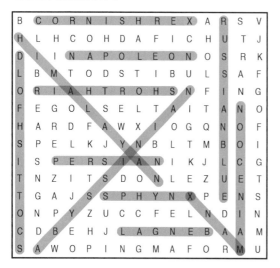

Bonus Answer: cat breeds

WORD SEARCH 2

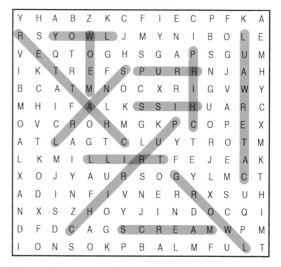

Bonus Answer: sounds cats make

SOLUTIONS

WHAT'S DIFFERENT? 1

1. lumps on the canvas bag
2. banana
3. fruit/vegetable the cat is holding
4. round stud earring
5. number of tail stripes
6. zig-zag stripe on bag
7. lemons vs. butternut squash
8. socks

WHAT'S DIFFERENT? 2

1. facemask fill pattern
2. extra fish over cat tail
3. eel
4. flipper tips
5. fin on the Copperband Butterflyfish
6. pattern on the oxygen tank
7. bubbles from mask
8. fill pattern on the coral

SOLUTIONS

WORD SCRAMBLE

1. your face
2. windowsill
3. kitchen table
4. computer
5. couch
6. in the air
7. countertop
8. your plate
9. pillow
10. cardboard box

FIND THE DIFFERENT CAT

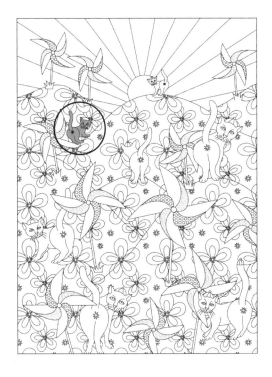

SOLUTIONS

MAZE 1

MAZE 2

Val Brains is an author/illustrator and humorist.

Val believes that laughter and coloring are for everyone. Her goal is to bring you funny and unique Cat Butt illustrations to color, gift, and chortle at together. She loves reading your reviews, especially your stories about how Cat Butts brightened someone's day, helped them through a difficult time, or crushed all the other gifts at the office holiday party. Honestly, the bad reviews are entertaining too.

You can see more of Val's work on Instagram @valbrains and at valbrains.com. For the latest on Val's Cat Butt Coloring Books, also follow @catbuttcoloring on Instagram.